SURSUM CORDA

SELECTED POEMS OF
CLAUDE McKAY

SELECTED POEMS OF

CLAUDE McKAY

WITH A BIOGRAPHICAL NOTE BY

Max Eastman

A Harvest/HBJ Book
Harcourt Brace Jovanovich, Publishers
San Diego   New York   London

CONTENTS

BIOGRAPHICAL NOTE

by MAX EASTMAN

CLAUDE MCKAY was most widely known perhaps as a novelist, author of *Home to Harlem,* a national best-seller in 1928. But he will live in history as the first great lyric genius that his race produced.

He was a full-blooded African, of middle height and dark chestnut color. In feature and expression he strangely resembled a portrait of King Christopher of Haiti that was published many years ago in the *London Illustrated News.* His eyebrows arched high up and never came down, and his finely modelled features wore in consequence a fixed expression of ironical and rather mischievous scepticism. Claude *was* ironical and mischievous too, and acutely intelligent both about people and politics. His laughter at the frailties of his friends and enemies, no matter which—that high, half-wailing falsetto laugh of the recklessly delighted Darky—was the center of my joy in him throughout our friendship of more than thirty years.

Claude was born in 1890 in a little thatched farm house of two rooms in the hilly middle country of Jamaica in the West Indies. He learned in childhood how a family of his ancestors, brought over in chains from Madagascar, had kept together by declaring a death strike on the auction block. Each would kill himself. they vowed solemnly, if they were sold to separate owners. With the blood of such rebels in his veins, and their memory to stir it, Claude McKay grew up proud of his race and with no disposition to apologize for his color.

In his homeland they call him "Jamaica's Bobbie Burns," and there is some reason for this. In both poets the defiant pride of the social rebel, the militant democrat, while nobly expressed, is on the whole overborne by a mood of all-embracing human tenderness. The sonnet "If We Must Die," in which he confronts the lynchers, is his most popular poem among the Negroes. But "Harlem Shadows," the poem of pure compassion which first brought him attention in America, is a better lyric. And the sonnet he called "Baptism" is, I think, as fine an expression of the courage to endure anguish and grow stronger by it as we have in our language.

Claude McKay came to America in 1912, and attended the Agricultural College of Kansas. His intention was to learn scientific farming and return to Jamaica to offer practical wisdom as well as song to his people. He studied for two years in Kansas, thinking continually less about farming and more about literature, and gradually losing out of mind the idea of returning to Jamaica. He left the college in 1914, knowing that he was a poet—and imagining, I guess, that he was a rather irresponsible and wayward character—to cast in his lot with the working-class Negroes of our North. He earned his living in every one of the ways the northern Negroes do, from pot-wrestling in a boarding-house kitchen to dining-car service on the New York and Washington express. But like most poets he failed to take earning a living very seriously. It was a matter of collecting enough money from each new job to quit for a while and sing. He was often homesick for Jamaica, and some of his best songs are made of the bright images that crowded in when he thought of his childhood home. Like a bluebird's note in a March wind, those sudden clear thoughts of the warm South ring out in the midst of his northern songs. "Oh something must be happening there this very minute!" Underlying them all, I suppose, is a yearning for his wise and gentle mother, the moment of whose death he conveys into our heart with a simplicity that belongs only to the rarest of earth's wonders, the true-born lyric poet.

His poems led to our meeting, and in a few years he became my associate editor on *The Liberator,* a socialist magazine of art and literature. We were together in Moscow in 1923, both sympathetic to the Bolshevik Revolution, both unofficial visitors, however, and not fanatical. There being no Negroes in Russia, and one very much needed to demonstrate the new race solidarity, Claude was taken up—and played up—to a degree that would have turned the head of anyone not endowed at birth with those sceptical eyebrows. Adopted as a kind of mascot by the Red Army and Navy, entertained everywhere at the state's expense, given a Grand Duke's bedroom and study to live and work in, exhibited on tribunes with the great leaders and orators of the revolution, Claude certainly had the time of his life.

But his mind was in command. He saw clearly the authoritarian mechanism behind these "spontaneous" demonstrations, the regimentation, the bigotry, the sacrifice of personal dignity to the momentary needs of the state. In midstream of that flood of officially sponsored adulation in which a less independent mind would have gone down, he composed a sonnet to St. Isaac's Church in Petrograd, which asserts in sublime opposition to the whole trend and essence of it the divinity of the individual man.

After a year in Russia Claude went back to France and down to Morocco to live quietly and write books that had little to do with socialism. But he did not conceal his contempt for the increasingly ruthless tyranny over man's mind and body that he saw growing out of the great revolution that had lifted him so high. He was not sucked in by the "racial democracy" for which so many of Stalin's American fellow-travelers were willing to trade the substance of freedom for any man, black or white.

His last years were passed in sickness; he could not write much; and he was destitute. One word on the communist side would have brought him ease, comfort, contemporary fame and a good income. But he would not speak it. He chose instead to live in penury, and watch his fame and popularity gradually disappear from the earth. A few years more and he would have seen them rise again, for his choice was as correct as it was courageous, and his place in the world's literature is unique and is assured.

THE WORD

Oh spread Thy words like green fields, watered,
fresh,
The Word is God and the Word is made flesh!

SONGS FOR JAMAICA

FLAME-HEART

So much I have forgotten in ten years,
So much in ten brief years! I have forgot
What time the purple apples come to juice,
And what month brings the shy forget-me-not.
I have forgot the special, startling season
Of the pimento's flowering and fruiting;
What time of year the ground doves brown the fields
And fill the noonday with their curious fluting.
I have forgotten much, but still remember
The poinsettia's red, blood-red, in warm December.

I still recall the honey-fever grass,
But cannot recollect the high days when
We rooted them out of the ping-wing path
To stop the mad bees in the rabbit pen.
I often try to think in what sweet month
The languid painted ladies used to dapple
The yellow by-road mazing from the main,
Sweet with the golden threads of the rose-apple.
I have forgotten—strange—but quite remember
The poinsettia's red, blood-red, in warm December.

What weeks, what months, what time of the mild year
We cheated school to have our fling at tops?
What days our wine-thrilled bodies pulsed with joy
Feasting upon blackberries in the copse?
Oh some I know! I have embalmed the days,
Even the sacred moments when we played,
All innocent of passion, uncorrupt,
At noon and evening in the flame-heart's shade.
We were so happy, happy, I remember,
Beneath the poinsettia's red in warm December.

THE EASTER FLOWER

Far from this foreign Easter damp and chilly
    My soul steals to a pear-shaped plot of ground
Where gleamed the lilac-tinted Easter Lily
    Soft-scented in the air for yards around;

Alone, without a hint of guardian leaf!
    Just like a fragile bell of silver rime,
It burst the tomb for freedom sweet and brief
    In the young pregnant year at Eastertime;

And many thought it was a sacred sign,
    And some called it the resurrection flower;
And I, in wonder, worshiped at its shrine,
    Yielding my heart unto its perfumed power.

SPRING IN NEW HAMPSHIRE

(To J. L. J. F. E.)

Too green the springing April grass,
   Too blue the silver-speckled sky,
For me to linger here, alas,
   While happy winds go laughing by,
Wasting the golden hours indoors,
Washing windows and scrubbing floors.

Too wonderful the April night,
   Too faintly sweet the first May flowers,
The stars too gloriously bright,
   For me to spend the evening hours,
When fields are fresh and streams are leaping,
Wearied, exhausted, dully sleeping.

SUMMER MORN IN NEW HAMPSHIRE

All yesterday it poured, and all night long
    I could not sleep; the rain unceasing beat
Upon the shingled roof like a weird song,
    Upon the grass like running children's feet.
And down the mountains by the dark cloud kissed,
    Like a strange shape in filmy veiling dressed,
Slid slowly, silently, the wraith-like mist,
    And nestled soft against the earth's wet breast.

But lo, there was a miracle at dawn!
    The still air stirred at touch of the faint breeze,
The sun a sheet of gold bequeathed the lawn,
    The songsters twittered in the rustling trees.
And all things were transfigured in the day,
    But me whom radiant beauty could not move;
For you, more wonderful, were far away,
    And I was blind with hunger for your love.

SUKEE RIVER

Thou sweet-voiced stream that first gavest me drink,
    Watched o'er me when I floated on thy breast;
What black-faced boy now gambols on thy brink,
    Or finds beneath thy rocks a place of rest?
What naked lad doth linger long by thee,
    And run and tumble in the sun-scorched sand,
Or heed the pea-dove in the wild fig tree,
    While I am roaming in an alien land?
No wonder that my heart is happy never,
    For I've been faithless to thee, Sukee River.

        I shall love you ever,
        Dearest Sukee River:
      Dash against my broken heart,
      Nevermore from you I'll part;
        But will stay for ever,
        Crystal Sukee River.

HOMING SWALLOWS

Swift swallows sailing from the Spanish main,
    O rain-birds racing merrily away
From hill-tops parched with heat and sultry plain
    Of wilting plants and fainting flowers, say—

When at the noon hour from the chapel school
    The children dash and scamper down the dale,
Scornful of teacher's rod and binding rule
    Forever broken and without avail,

Do they still stop beneath the giant tree
    To gather locusts in their childish greed,
And chuckle when they break the pods to see
    The golden powder clustered round the seed?

TO ONE COMING NORTH

At first you'll joy to see the playful snow,
    Like white moths trembling on the tropic air,
Or waters of the hills that softly flow
    Gracefully falling down a shining stair.

And when the fields and streets are covered white,
    And the wind-worried void is chilly, raw;
Or underneath a spell of heat and light
    The cheerless frozen spots begin to thaw,

Like me you'll long for home, where birds' glad song
    Means flowering lanes and leas and spaces dry,
And tender thoughts and feelings fine and strong,
    Beneath a vivid, silver-flecked, blue sky.

But oh! more than the changeless southern isles,
    When Spring has shed upon the earth her charm,
You'll love the Northland wreathed in golden smiles
    By the miraculous sun turned glad and warm.

O sweet are tropic lands for waking dreams!
　　There time and life move lazily along.
There by the banks of blue and silver streams
　　Grass-sheltered crickets chirp incessant song;
Gay-colored lizards loll all through the day,
　　Their tongues outstretched for careless little flies.

And swarthy children in the fields at play,
　　Look upward, laughing at the smiling skies.
A breath of idleness is in the air
　　That casts a subtle spell upon all things,
And love and mating-time are everywhere,
　　And wonder to life's commonplaces clings.

The fluttering humming-bird darts through the trees,
　　And dips his long beak in the big bell-flowers.
The leisured buzzard floats upon the breeze,
　　Riding a crescent cloud for endless hours.
The sea beats softly on the emerald strands—
　　O sweet for quiet dreams are tropic lands!

HOME THOUGHTS

Oh something just now must be happening there!
That suddenly and quiveringly here,
Amid the city's noises, I must think
Of mangoes leaning to the river's brink,
And dexterous Davie climbing high above,
The gold fruits ebon-speckled to remove,
And toss them quickly in the tangled mass
Of wis-wis twisted round the guinea grass.
And Cyril coming through the bramble-track
A prize bunch of bananas on his back;
And Georgie—none could ever dive like him—
Throwing his scanty clothes off for a swim;
And schoolboys, from Bridge-tunnel going home,
Watching the waters downward dash and foam.
This is no daytime dream, there's something in it,
Oh something's happening there this very minute!

Reg wished me to go with him to the field.
I paused because I did not want to go;
But in her quiet way she made me yield,
Reluctantly, for she was breathing low.
Her hand she slowly lifted from her lap
And, smiling sadly in the old sweet way,
She pointed to the nail where hung my cap.
Her eyes said: I shall last another day.
But scarcely had we reached the distant place,
When over the hills we heard a faint bell ringing.
A boy came running up with frightened face—
We knew the fatal news that he was bringing.
I heard him listlessly, without a moan,
Although the only one I loved was gone.

II

The dawn departs, the morning is begun,
The Trades come whispering from off the seas,
The fields of corn are golden in the sun,
The dark-brown tassels fluttering in the breeze;
The bell is sounding and children pass,
Frog-leaping, skipping, shouting, laughing shrill,
Down the red road, over the pasture-grass,
Up to the schoolhouse crumbling on the hill.
The older folk are at their peaceful toil,
Some pulling up the weeds, some plucking corn,
And others breaking up the sun-baked soil.
Float, faintly-scented breeze, at early morn
Over the earth where mortals sow and reap—
Beneath its breast my mother lies asleep.

DECEMBER, 1919

Last night I heard your voice, mother,
    The words you sang to me
When I, a little barefoot boy,
    Knelt down against your knee.

And tears gushed from my heart, mother,
    And passed beyond its wall,
But though the fountain reached my throat
    The drops refused to fall.

'Tis ten years since you died, mother,
    Just ten dark years of pain,
And oh, I only wish that I
    Could weep just once again.

THE SPANISH NEEDLE

Lovely dainty Spanish needle
 With your yellow flower and white,
Dew-bedecked and softly sleeping,
 Do you think of me tonight?

Shadowed by the spreading mango,
 Nodding by the rippling stream,
Tell me, dear plant of my childhood,
 Do you of the exile dream?

Do you see me by the brookside,
 Catching crabs beneath the stone?
As you did the day you whispered:
 Leave the harmless dears alone?

Do you see me in the meadow,
 Coming from the woodland spring,
With a bamboo on my shoulder
 And a pail slung from a string?

Do you see me all expectant,
 Lying in an orange grove,
While the swee-swees sing above me,
 Waiting for my elf-eyed love?

Lovely dainty Spanish needle,
 Source to me of sweet delight,
In your far-off sunny southland
 Do you dream of me to-night?

THE PLATEAU

It was the silver, heart-enveloping view
    Of the mysterious sea-line far away,
    Seen only on a gleaming gold-white day,
That made it dear and beautiful to you.

And Laura loved it for the little hill,
    Where the quartz sparkled fire, barren and dun,
    Whence in the shadow of the dying sun,
She contemplated Hallow's wooden mill.

While Danny liked the sheltering high grass,
    In which he lay upon a clear dry night,
    To hear and see, screened skilfully from sight,
The happy lovers of the valley pass.

But oh! I loved it for the big round moon
    That swung out of the clouds and swooned aloft,
    Burning with passion, gloriously soft,
Lighting the purple flowers of fragrant June.

WILD MAY

Aleta mentions in her tender letters,
Among a chain of quaint and touching things,
That you are feeble, weighted down with fetters,
And given to strange deeds and mutterings.
No longer without trace or thought of fear,
Do you leap to and ride the rebel roan;
But have become the victim of grim care,
With three brown beauties to support alone.
But none the less will you be in my mind,
Wild May that cantered by the risky ways,
With showy head-cloth flirting in the wind,
From market in the glad December days;
Wild May of whom even other girls could rave
Before sex tamed your spirit, made you slave.

ADOLESCENCE

There was a time when in late afternoon
    The four-o'clocks would fold up at day's close,
Pink-white in prayer. Under the floating moon
    I lay with them in calm and sweet repose.

And in the open spaces I could sleep,
    Half-naked to the shining worlds above;
Peace came with sleep and sleep was long and deep,
    Gained without effort, sweet like early love.

But now no balm—nor drug nor weed nor wine—
    Can bring true rest to cool my body's fever,
Nor sweeten in my mouth the acrid brine,
    That salts my choicest drink and will forever.

THE WILD GOAT

O you would clothe me in silken frocks
    And house me from the cold,
And bind with bright bands my glossy locks,
    And buy me chains of gold.

And give me, meekly to do my will,
    The hapless sons of men;
But the wild goat bounding on the barren hill
    Droops in the grassy pen.

HERITAGE

Now the dead past seems vividly alive,
    And in this shining moment I can trace,
Down through the vista of the vanished years,
    Your faun-like form, your fond elusive face.

And suddenly some secret spring's released,
    And unawares a riddle is revealed,
And I can read like large, black-lettered print,
    What seemed before a thing forever sealed.

I know the magic word, the graceful thought,
    The song that fills me in my lucid hours,
The spirit's wine that thrills my body through,
    And makes me music-drunk, are yours, all yours.

I cannot praise, for you have passed from praise,
    I have no tinted thought to paint you true;
But I can feel and I can write the word:
    The best of me is but the least of you.

AFTER THE WINTER

Some day, when trees have shed their leaves
  And against the morning's white
The shivering birds beneath the eaves
  Have sheltered for the night,
We'll turn our faces southward, love,
  Toward the summer isle
Where bamboos spire the shafted grove
  And wide-mouthed orchids smile.

And we will seek the quiet hill
  Where towers the cotton tree,
And leaps the laughing crystal rill,
  And works the droning bee.
And we will build a cottage there
  Beside an open glade,
With black-ribbed blue-bells blowing near,
  And ferns that never fade.

THE TROPICS IN NEW YORK

Bananas ripe and green, and ginger-root,
    Cocoa in pods and alligator pears,
And tangerines and mangoes and grape fruit,
    Fit for the highest prize at parish fairs,

Set in the window, bringing memories
    Of fruit-trees laden by low-singing rills,
And dewy dawns, and mystical blue skies
    In benediction over nun-like hills.

My eyes grew dim, and I could no more gaze;
    A wave of longing through my body swept,
And, hungry for the old, familiar ways,
    I turned aside and bowed my head and wept.

I SHALL RETURN

I shall return again. I shall return
To laugh and love and watch with wonder-eyes
At golden noon the forest fires burn,
Wafting their blue-black smoke to sapphire skies.
I shall return to loiter by the streams
That bathe the brown blades of the bending grasses,
And realize once more my thousand dreams
Of waters rushing down the mountain passes.
I shall return to hear the fiddle and fife
Of village dances, dear delicious tunes
That stir the hidden depths of native life,
Stray melodies of dim-remembered runes.
I shall return. I shall return again
To ease my mind of long, long years of pain.

BAPTISM

BAPTISM

Into the furnace let me go alone;
Stay you without in terror of the heat.
I will go naked in—for thus 'tis sweet—
Into the weird depths of the hottest zone.
I will not quiver in the frailest bone,
You will not note a flicker of defeat;
My heart shall tremble not its fate to meet,
My mouth give utterance to any moan.
The yawning oven spits forth fiery spears;
Red aspish tongues shout wordlessly my name.
Desire destroys, consumes my mortal fears,
Transforming me into a shape of flame.
I will come out, back to your world of tears,
A stronger soul within a finer frame.

IF WE MUST DIE

If we must die, let it not be like hogs
Hunted and penned in an inglorious spot,
While round us bark the mad and hungry dogs,
Making their mock at our accursed lot.
If we must die, O let us nobly die,
So that our precious blood may not be shed
In vain; then even the monsters we defy
Shall be constrained to honor us though dead!
O kinsmen! we must meet the common foe!
Though far outnumbered let us show us brave,
And for their thousand blows deal one deathblow!
What though before us lies the open grave?
Like men we'll face the murderous, cowardly pack,
Pressed to the wall, dying, but fighting back!

THE LYNCHING

His Spirit in smoke ascended to high heaven.
His father, by the cruelest way of pain,
Had bidden him to his bosom once again;
The awful sin remained still unforgiven.
All night a bright and solitary star
(Perchance the one that ever guided him,
Yet gave him up at last to Fate's wild whim)
Hung pitifully o'er the swinging char.
Day dawned, and soon the mixed crowds came to
    view
The ghastly body swaying in the sun.
The women thronged to look, but never a one
Showed sorrow in her eyes of steely blue.

And little lads, lynchers that were to be,
Danced round the dreadful thing in fiendish glee.

TO THE WHITE FIENDS

Think you I am not fiend and savage too?
Think you I could not arm me with a gun
And shoot down ten of you for every one
Of my black brothers murdered, burnt by you?
Be not deceived, for every deed you do
I could match—out-match: am I not Afric's son,
Black of that black land where black deeds are done?
But the Almighty from the darkness drew
My soul and said: Even thou shalt be a light
Awhile to burn on the benighted earth,
Thy dusky face I set among the white
For thee to prove thyself of higher worth;
Before the world is swallowed up in night,
To show thy little lamp: go forth, go forth!

IN BONDAGE

I would be wandering in distant fields
Where man, and bird, and beast, lives leisurely,
And the old earth is kind, and ever yields
Her goodly gifts to all her children free;
Where life is fairer, lighter, less demanding,
And boys and girls have time and space for play
Before they come to years of understanding—
Somewhere I would be singing, far away.
For life is greater than the thousand wars
Men wage for it in their insatiate lust,
And will remain like the eternal stars,
When all that shines to-day is drift and dust.

But I am bound with you in your mean graves,
O black men, simple slaves of ruthless slaves.

AFRICA

The sun sought thy dim bed and brought forth light,
The sciences were sucklings at thy breast;
When all the world was young in pregnant night
Thy slaves toiled at thy monumental best.
Thou ancient treasure-land, thou modern prize,
New peoples marvel at thy pyramids!
The years roll on, thy sphinx of riddle eyes
Watches the mad world with immobile lids.
The Hebrews humbled them at Pharaoh's name.
Cradle of Power! Yet all things were in vain!
Honor and Glory, Arrogance and Fame!
They went. The darkness swallowed thee again.
Thou art the harlot, now thy time is done,
Of all the mighty nations of the sun.

OUTCAST

For the dim regions whence my fathers came
My spirit, bondaged by the body, longs.
Words felt, but never heard, my lips would frame;
My soul would sing forgotten jungle songs.
I would go back to darkness and to peace,
But the great western world holds me in fee,
And I may never hope for full release
While to its alien gods I bend my knee.
Something in me is lost, forever lost,
Some vital thing has gone out of my heart,
And I must walk the way of life a ghost
Among the sons of earth, a thing apart.

For I was born, far from my native clime,
Under the white man's menace, out of time.

ENSLAVED

Oh when I think of my long-suffering race,
For weary centuries, despised, oppressed
Enslaved and lynched, denied a human place
In the great life line of the Christian West;
And in the Black Land disinherited,
Robbed in the ancient country of its birth,
My heart grows sick with hate, becomes as lead,
For this my race that has no home on earth.
Then from the dark depth of my soul I cry
To the avenging angel to consume
The white man's world of wonders utterly:
Let it be swallowed up in earth's vast womb,
Or upward roll as sacrificial smoke
To liberate my people from its yoke!

O WORD I LOVE TO SING

O word I love to sing! thou art too tender
　　For all the passions agitating me;
For all my bitterness thou art too tender,
　　I cannot pour my red soul into thee.

O haunting melody! thou art too slender,
　　Too fragile like a globe of crystal glass;
For all my stormy thoughts thou art too slender,
　　The burden from my bosom will not pass.

O tender word! O melody so slender!
　　O tears of passion saturate with brine,
O words, unwilling words, ye can not render
　　My hatred for the foe of me and mine.

LOOK WITHIN

Lord, let me not be silent while we fight
    In Europe Germans, Asia Japanese
For setting up a Fascist way of might
    While fifteen million Negroes on their knees
Pray for salvation from the Fascist yoke
    Of these United States. Remove the beam
(Nearly two thousand years since Jesus spoke)
    From your own eyes before the mote you deem
It proper from your neighbor's to extract!
    We bathe our lies in vapors of sweet myrrh,
And close our eyes not to perceive the fact!
    But Jesus said: You whited sepulchre,
Pretending to be uncorrupt of sin,
    While worm-infested, rotten through within!

LIKE A STRONG TREE

Like a strong tree that in the virgin earth
Sends far its roots through rock and loam and clay,
And proudly thrives in rain or time of dearth,
When dry waves scare the rain-come sprites away;
Like a strong tree that reaches down deep, deep,
For sunken water, fluid underground,
Where the great-ringed unsightly blind worms creep,
And queer things of the nether world abound:
So would I live in rich imperial growth,
Touching the surface and the depth of things,
Instinctively responsive unto both,
Tasting the sweets of being, fearing no stings,
Sensing the subtle spell of changing forms,
Like a strong tree against a thousand storms.

TRUTH

Lord, shall I find it in Thy Holy Church,
Or must I give it up as something dead,
Forever lost, no matter where I search,
Like dinosaurs within their ancient bed?
I found it not in years of Unbelief,
In science stirring life like budding trees,
In Revolution like a dazzling thief—
Oh, shall I find it on my bended knees?

But what is Truth? So Pilate asked Thee, Lord,
So long ago when Thou wert manifest,
As the Eternal and Incarnate Word,
Chosen of God and by Him singly blest:
In this vast world of lies and hate and greed,
Upon my knees, Oh Lord, for Truth I plead.

TIGER

The white man is a tiger at my throat,
Drinking my blood as my life ebbs away,
And muttering that his terrible striped coat
Is Freedom's and portends the Light of Day.
Oh white man, you may suck up all my blood
And throw my carcass into potter's field,
But never will I say with you that mud
Is bread for Negroes! Never will I yield.

Europe and Africa and Asia wait
The touted New Deal of the New World's hand!
New systems will be built on race and hate,
The Eagle and the Dollar will command.
Oh Lord! My body, and my heart too, break—
The tiger in his strength his thirst must slake!

Oh, One was black of the wise men of the East,
Who came with precious gifts to Jesus' birth,
A symbol all men equal were at least,
When Godhead condescended to the earth.
The Ethiopian in Jerusalem
Was human to the preacher of our Lord,
Who drawn to him as to a precious gem,
Bestowed on him the message of the Word.

Yes, and a great Black Empire was the first,
To change itself into a Christian nation,
Long before Rome its pagan fetters burst
And purged itself for Jesus Christ's oblation.
From the high place where erstwhile they grew drunk
With power, oh God, how gutter-low have black men
    sunk!

THE PAGAN ISMS

Around me roar and crash the pagan isms
To which most of my life was consecrate,
Betrayed by evil men and torn by schisms
For they were built on nothing more than hate!
I cannot live my life without the faith
Where new sensations like a fawn will leap,
But old enthusiasms like a wraith,
Haunt me awake and haunt me when I sleep.

And so to God I go to make my peace,
Where black nor white can follow to betray.
My pent-up heart to Him I will release
And surely He will show the perfect way
Of life. For He will lead me and no man
Can violate or circumvent His plan.

THE NEGRO'S TRAGEDY

It is the Negro's tragedy I feel
Which binds me like a heavy iron chain,
It is the Negro's wounds I want to heal
Because I know the keenness of his pain.
Only a thorn-crowned Negro and no white
Can penetrate into the Negro's ken,
Or feel the thickness of the shroud of night
Which hides and buries him from other men.

So what I write is urged out of my blood.
There is no white man who could write my book,
Though many think their story should be told
Of what the Negro people ought to brook.
Our statesmen roam the world to set things right.
This Negro laughs and prays to God for Light!

THE NEGRO'S FRIEND

There is no radical the Negro's friend
Who points some other than the classic road
For him to follow, fighting to the end,
Thinking to ease him of one half his load.
What waste of time to cry: "No Segregation!"
When it exists in stark reality,
Both North and South, throughout this total nation,
The state decreed by white authority.

Must fifteen million blacks be gratified,
That one of them can enter as a guest,
A fine white house—the rest of them denied
A place of decent sojourn and a rest?
Oh, Segregation is not the whole sin,
The Negroes need salvation from within.

THE DESOLATE CITY

My spirit is a pestilential city,
With misery triumphant everywhere,
Glutted with baffled hopes and human pity.
Strange agonies make quiet lodgement there:
Its sewers, bursting, ooze up from below
And spread their loathsome substance through its lanes,
Flooding all areas with their evil flow
And blocking all the motions of its veins:
Its life is sealed to love or hope or pity,
My spirit is a pestilential city.

Above its walls the air is heavy-wet,
Brooding in fever mood and hanging thick
Round empty tower and broken minaret,
Settling upon the tree tops stricken sick
And withered under its contagious breath.
Their leaves are shrivelled silver, parched decay,
Like wilting creepers trailing underneath
The chalky yellow of a tropic way.
Round crumbling tower and leaning minaret,
The air hangs fever-filled and heavy-wet.

And all its many fountains no more spurt;
Within the dammed-up tubes they tide and foam,
Around the drifted sludge and silted dirt,
And weep against the soft and liquid loam.
And so the city's ways are washed no more,
All is neglected and decayed within,
Clean waters beat against its high-walled shore
In furious force, but cannot enter in:
The suffocated fountains cannot spurt,
They foam and rage against the silted dirt.

Beneath the ebon gloom of mounting rocks
The little pools lie poisonously still,
And birds come to the edge in forlorn flocks,
And utter sudden, plaintive notes and shrill,
Pecking at strangely gray-green substances;
But never do they dip their bills and drink.
They twitter, sad beneath the mournful trees,
And fretfully flit to and from the brink,
In little gray-brown, green-and-purple flocks,
Beneath the jet-gloom of the mounting rocks.

And green-eyed moths of curious design,
With gold-black wings and rarely silver-dotted,
On nests of flowers among those rocks recline,
Bold, burning blossoms, strangely leopard-spotted,
But breathing deadly poison from their lips.
And every lovely moth that wanders by,
And from the blossoms fatal nectar sips,
Is doomed to drooping stupor, there to die;
All green-eyed moths of curious design
That on the fiercely-burning blooms recline.

Oh cold as death is all the loveliness,
That breathes out of the strangeness of the scene,
And sickening like a skeleton's caress,
Of clammy clinging fingers, long and lean.
Above it float a host of yellow flies,
Circling in changeless motion in their place,
That came down snow-thick from the freighted skies,
Swarming across the gluey floor of space:
Oh cold as death is all the loveliness,
And sickening like a skeleton's caress.

There was a time when, happy with the birds,
The little children clapped their hands and laughed;
And midst the clouds the glad winds heard their words
And blew down all the merry ways to waft
The music through the scented fields of flowers.
Oh sweet were children's voices in those days,
Before the fall of pestilential showers,
That drove them forth far from the city's ways:
Now never, nevermore their silver words
Will mingle with the golden of the birds.

Gone, gone forever the familiar forms
To which the city once so dearly clung,
Blown worlds beyond by the destroying storms
And lost away like lovely songs unsung.
Yet life still lingers, questioningly strange,
Timid and quivering, naked and alone,
Against the cycle of disruptive change,
Though all the fond familiar forms are gone,
Forever gone, the fond familiar forms;
Blown worlds beyond by the destroying storms.

A PRAYER

'Mid the discordant noises of the day I hear thee calling;
I stumble as I fare along Earth's way; keep me from falling.

Mine eyes are open but they cannot see for gloom of night;
I can no more than lift my heart to thee for inward light.

The wild and fiery passion of my youth consumes my soul;
In agony I turn to thee for truth and self-control.

For Passion and all the pleasures it can give will die the death;
But this of me eternally must live, thy borrowed breath.

'Mid the discordant noises of the day I hear thee calling;
I stumble as I fare along Earth's way; keep me from falling.

I KNOW MY SOUL

I plucked my soul out of its secret place,
And held it to the mirror of my eye,
To see it like a star against the sky,
A twitching body quivering in space,
A spark of passion shining on my face.
And I explored it to determine why
This awful key to my infinity
Conspires to rob me of sweet joy and grace.
And if the sign may not be fully read,
If I can comprehend but not control,
I need not gloom my days with futile dread,
Because I see a part and not the whole.
Contemplating the strange, I'm comforted
By this narcotic thought: I know my soul.

AMERICANA

AMERICA

Although she feeds me bread of bitterness,
And sinks into my throat her tiger's tooth,
Stealing my breath of life, I will confess
I love this cultured hell that tests my youth!
Her vigor flows like tides into my blood,
Giving me strength erect against her hate.
Her bigness sweeps my being like a flood.
Yet as a rebel fronts a king in state,
I stand within her walls with not a shred
Of terror, malice, not a word of jeer.
Darkly I gaze into the days ahead,
And see her might and granite wonders there,
Beneath the touch of Time's unerring hand,
Like priceless treasures sinking in the sand.

HARLEM SHADOWS

I hear the halting footsteps of a lass
    In Negro Harlem when the night lets fall
Its veil. I see the shapes of girls who pass
    To bend and barter at desire's call.
Ah, little dark girls who in slippered feet
Go prowling through the night from street to street!

Through the long night until the silver break
    Of day the little gray feet know no rest;
Through the lone night until the last snow-flake
    Has dropped from heaven upon the earth's
        white breast,
The dusky, half-clad girls of tired feet
Are trudging, thinly shod, from street to street.

Ah, stern harsh world, that in the wretched way
    Of poverty, dishonor and disgrace,
Has pushed the timid little feet of clay,
    The sacred brown feet of my fallen race!
Ah, heart of me, the weary, weary feet
In Harlem wandering from street to street.

THE HARLEM DANCER

Applauding youths laughed with young prostitutes
And watched her perfect, half-clothed body sway;
Her voice was like the sound of blended flutes
Blown by black players upon a picnic day.
She sang and danced on gracefully and calm,
The light gauze hanging loose about her form;
To me she seemed a proudly-swaying palm
Grown lovelier for passing through a storm.
Upon her swarthy neck black shiny curls
Luxuriant fell; and tossing coins in praise,
The wine-flushed, bold-eyed boys, and even the girls,
Devoured her shape with eager, passionate gaze;
But looking at her falsely-smiling face,
I knew her self was not in that strange place.

The tired cars go grumbling by,
    The moaning, groaning cars,
And the old milk carts go rumbling by
    Under the same dull stars.
Out of the tenements, cold as stone,
    Dark figures start for work;
I watch them sadly shuffle on,
    'Tis dawn, dawn in New York.

    But I would be on the island of the sea,
    In the heart of the island of the sea,
Where the cocks are crowing, crowing, crowing,
    And the hens are cackling in the rose-apple tree,
Where the old draft-horse is neighing, neighing, neighing
    Out on the brown dew-silvered lawn,
    And the tethered cow is lowing, lowing, lowing,
And dear old Ned is braying, braying, braying,
And the shaggy Nannie goat is calling, calling, calling
    From her little trampled corner of the long wide lea
That stretches to the waters of the hill-stream falling
    Sheer upon the flat rocks joyously!
    There, oh there! on the island of the sea,
        There would I be at dawn.

The tired cars go grumbling by,
    The crazy, lazy cars,
And the same milk carts go rumbling by
    Under the dying stars.
A lonely newsboy hurries by,
    Humming a recent ditty;
Red streaks strike through the gray of the sky,
    The dawn comes to the city.

But I would be on the island of the sea,
    In the heart of the island of the sea,
Where the cocks are crowing, crowing, crowing,
    And the hens are cackling in the rose-apple tree,
Where the old draft-horse is neighing, neighing, neighing
    Out on the brown dew-silvered lawn,
    And the tethered cow is lowing, lowing, lowing,
And dear old Ned is braying, braying, braying,
And the shaggy Nannie goat is calling, calling, calling
    From her little trampled corner of the long wide lea
That stretches to the waters of the hill-stream falling
    Sheer upon the flat rocks joyously!
    There, oh there! on the island of the sea,
        There would I be at dawn.

ON THE ROAD

Roar of the rushing train fearfully rocking,
Impatient people jammed in line for food,
The rasping noise of cars together knocking,
And worried waiters, some in ugly mood,
Crowding into the choking pantry hole
To call out dishes for each angry glutton
Exasperated grown beyond control,
From waiting for his soup or fish or mutton.
At last the station's reached, the engine stops;
For bags and wraps the red-caps circle round;
From off the step the passenger lightly hops,
And seeks his cab or tram-car homeward bound;
The waiters pass out weary, listless, glum,
To spend their tips on harlots, cards and rum.

DAWN IN NEW YORK

The Dawn! The Dawn! The crimson-tinted, comes
Out of the low still skies, over the hills,
Manhattan's roofs and spires and cheerless domes!
The Dawn! My spirit to its spirit thrills.
Almost the mighty city is asleep,
No pushing crowd, no tramping, tramping feet.
But here and there a few cars groaning creep
Along, above, and underneath the street,
Bearing their strangely-ghostly burdens by,
The women and the men of garish nights,
Their eyes wine-weakened and their clothes awry,
Grotesques beneath the strong electric lights.
The shadows wane. The Dawn comes to New York.
And I go darkly-rebel to my work.

THE CITY'S LOVE

For one brief golden moment rare like wine,
The gracious city swept across the line;
Oblivious of the color of my skin,
Forgetting that I was an alien guest,
She bent to me, my hostile heart to win,
Caught me in passion to her pillowy breast.
The great, proud city, seized with a strange love,
Bowed down for one flame hour my pride to prove.

ON BROADWAY

About me young and careless feet
Linger along the garish street;
    Above, a hundred shouting signs
Shed down their bright fantastic glow
    Upon the merry crowd and lines
Of moving carriages below.
Oh wonderful is Broadway—only
My heart, my heart is lonely.

Desire naked, linked with Passion,
Goes strutting by in brazen fashion;
    From playhouse, cabaret and inn
The rainbow lights of Broadway blaze
    All gay without, all glad within.
As in a dream I stand and gaze
At Broadway, shining Broadway—only
My heart, my heart is lonely.

FRENCH LEAVE

No servile little fear shall daunt my will
    This morning. I have courage steeled to say
I will be lazy, conqueringly still,
    I will not lose the hours in toil this day.

The roaring world without, careless of souls,
    Shall leave me to my placid dream of rest,
My four walls shield me from its shouting ghouls,
    And all its hates have fled my quiet breast.

And I will loll here resting, wide awake,
    Dead to the world of work, the world of love.
I laze contented just for dreaming's sake
    With not the slightest urge to think or move.

How tired unto death, how tired I was!
    Now for a day I put my burdens by,
And like a child amidst the meadow grass
    Under the southern sun, I languid lie

And feel the bed about me kindly deep,
    My strength ooze gently from my hollow bones,
My worried brain drift aimlessly to sleep,
    Like softening to a song of tuneless tones.

A SONG OF THE MOON

The moonlight breaks upon the city's domes,
And falls along cemented steel and stone,
Upon the grayness of a million homes,
Lugubrious in unchanging monotone.

Upon the clothes behind the tenement,
That hang like ghosts suspended from the lines,
Linking each flat, but to each indifferent,
Incongruous and strange the moonlight shines.

There is no magic from your presence here,
So moon, sad moon, tuck up your trailing robe,
Whose silver seems antique and too severe
Against the glow of one electric globe.

Go spill your beauty on the laughing faces
Of happy flowers that bloom a thousand hues,
Waiting on tiptoe in the wilding spaces,
To drink your wine mixed with sweet draughts of
    dews.

MORNING JOY

At night the wide and level stretch of wold,
Which at high noon had basked in quiet gold,
Far as the eye could see was ghostly white;
Dark was the night save for the snow's weird light.

I drew the shades far down, crept into bed;
Hearing the cold wind moaning overhead
Through the sad pines, my soul, catching its pain,
Went sorrowing with it across the plain.

At dawn, behold! the pall of night was gone,
Save where a few shrubs melancholy, lone,
Detained a fragile shadow. Golden-lipped
The laughing grasses heaven's sweet wine sipped.

The sun rose smiling by the river's breast,
And my soul, by his happy spirit blest,
Soared like a bird to greet him in the sky,
And drew out of his heart Eternity.

WINTER IN THE COUNTRY

Sweet Life! how lovely to be here
    And feel the soft sea-laden breeze
Strike my flushed face, the spruce's fair
    Free limbs to see, the lesser trees'

Bare hands to touch, the sparrow's cheep
    To heed, and watch his nimble flight
Above the short brown grass asleep.
    Love glorious in his friendly might,

Music that every heart could bless,
    And thoughts of life serene, divine,
Beyond my power to express,
    Crowd round this lifted heart of mine!

But oh! to leave this paradise
    For the city's dirty basement room,
Where, beauty hidden from the eyes,
    A table, bed, bureau and broom

In corner set, two crippled chairs
    All covered up with dust and grim
With hideousness and scars of years,
    And gaslight burning weird and dim,

Will welcome me . . . And yet, and yet
    This very wind, the winter birds,
The glory of the soft sunset,
    Come there to me in words.

TO WINTER

Stay, season of calm love and soulful snows!
There is a subtle sweetness in the sun,
The ripples on the stream's breast gaily run,
The wind more boisterously by me blows,
And each succeeding day now longer grows,
The birds a gladder music have begun,
The squirrel, full of mischief and of fun,
From maple's topmost branch the brown twig throws.
I read these pregnant signs, know what they mean:
I know, cool winter, you intend to go.
Oh stay! I fled a land where fields are green
Always, and palms wave gently to and fro,
And winds are balmy, blue brooks ever sheen,
To ease my heart of its impassioned woe.

THE CASTAWAYS

The vivid grass with visible delight
Springing triumphant from the pregnant earth,
The butterflies, and sparrows in brief flight
Dancing and chirping for the season's birth,
The dandelions and rare daffodils
That touch the deep-stirred heart with hands of gold,
The thrushes sending forth their joyous trills,—
Not these, not these did I at first behold!
But seated on the benches daubed with green,
The castaways of life, a few asleep,
Some withered women desolate and mean,
And over all, life's shadows dark and deep.
Moaning I turned away, for misery
I have the strength to bear but not to see.

THE WHITE CITY

I will not toy with it nor bend an inch.
Deep in the secret chambers of my heart
I muse my life-long hate, and without flinch
I bear it nobly as I live my part.
My being would be a skeleton, a shell,
If this dark Passion that fills my every mood,
And makes my heaven in the white world's hell,
Did not forever feed me vital blood.
I see the mighty city through a mist—
The strident trains that speed the goaded mass,
The poles and spires and towers vapor-kissed,
The fortressed port through which the great ships
      pass,
The tides, the wharves, the dens I contemplate,
Are sweet like wanton loves because I hate.

SUBWAY WIND

Far down, down through the city's great gaunt gut
 The gray train rushing bears the weary wind;
In the packed cars the fans the crowd's breath cut,
 Leaving the sick and heavy air behind.
And pale-cheeked children seek the upper door
 To give their summer jackets to the breeze;
Their laugh is swallowed in the deafening roar
 Of captive wind that moans for fields and seas;
Seas cooling warm where native schooners drift
 Through sleepy waters, while gulls wheel and
  sweep,
Waiting for windy waves the keels to lift
 Lightly among the islands of the deep;
Islands of lofty palm trees blooming white
 That lend their perfume to the tropic sea,
Where fields lie idle in the dew-drenched night,
 And the Trades float above them fresh and free.

ALFONSO, DRESSING TO WAIT AT TABLE

Alfonso is a handsome bronze-hued lad
    Of subtly-changing and surprising parts;
His moods are storms that frighten and make glad,
    His eyes were made to capture women's hearts.

Down in the glory-hole Alfonso sings
    An olden song of wine and clinking glasses
And riotous rakes; magnificently flings
    Gay kisses to imaginary lasses.

Alfonso's voice of mellow music thrills
    Our swaying forms and steals our hearts with joy;
And when he soars, his fine falsetto trills
    Are rarest notes of gold without alloy.

But, O Alfonso! wherefore do you sing
    Dream-songs of carefree men and ancient places?
Soon we shall be beset by clamouring
    Of hungry and importunate palefaces.

REST IN PEACE

No more for you the city's thorny ways,
    The ugly corners of the Negro belt;
The miseries and pains of these harsh days
    By you will never, never again be felt.

No more, if still you wander, will you meet
    With nights of unabating bitterness;
They cannot reach you in your safe retreat,
    The city's hate, the city's prejudice!

'Twas sudden—but your menial task is done,
    The dawn now breaks on you, the dark is over,
The sea is crossed, the longed-for port is won;
    Farewell, oh, fare you well! my friend and
        lover.

THE WHITE HOUSE[*]

Your door is shut against my tightened face,
And I am sharp as steel with discontent;
But I possess the courage and the grace
To bear my anger proudly and unbent.
The pavement slabs burn loose beneath my feet,
A chafing savage, down the decent street;
And passion rends my vitals as I pass,
Where boldly shines your shuttered door of glass.
Oh, I must search for wisdom every hour,
Deep in my wrathful bosom sore and raw,
And find in it the superhuman power
To hold me to the letter of your law!
Oh, I must keep my heart inviolate
Against the potent poison of your hate.

[*] "My title was symbolic . . . it had no reference to the official residence of the President of the United States. . . . The title 'White Houses' changed the whole symbolic intent and meaning of the poem, making it appear as if the burning ambition of the black malcontent was to enter white houses in general." Claude McKay: *A Long Way from Home* (1937), pp. 313-314.

THE TIRED WORKER

O whisper, O my soul! The afternoon
Is waning into evening, whisper soft!
Peace, O my rebel heart! for soon the moon
From out its misty veil will swing aloft!
Be patient, weary body, soon the night
Will wrap thee gently in her sable sheet,
And with a leaden sigh thou wilt invite
To rest thy tired hands and aching feet.
The wretched day was theirs, the night is mine;
Come tender sleep, and fold me to thy breast.
But what steals out the gray clouds red like wine?
O dawn! O dreaded dawn! O let me rest
Weary my veins, my brain, my life! Have pity!
No! Once again the harsh, the ugly city.

THE BARRIER

I must not gaze at them although
Your eyes are dawning day;
I must not watch you as you go
Your sun-illumined way.

I hear but I must never heed
The fascinating note,
Which, fluting like a river reed,
Comes from your trembling throat.

I must not see upon your face
Love's softly glowing spark;
For there's the barrier of race,
You're fair and I am dark.

DIFFERENT PLACES

MOSCOW

Moscow for many loving her was dead . . .
And yet I saw a bright Byzantine fair,
Of jewelled buildings, pillars, domes and spires
Of hues prismatic dazzling to the sight;
A glory painted on the Eastern air,
Of amorous sounding tones like passionate lyres;
All colors laughing richly their delight
And reigning over all the color red.

My memory bears engraved the high-walled Kremlin,
Of halls symbolic of the tiger will,
Of Czarist instruments of mindless law . . .
And often now my nerves throb with the thrill
When, in that gilded place, I felt and saw
The presence and the simple voice of Lenin.

ST. ISAAC'S CHURCH, PETROGRAD

Bow down my soul in worship very low
And in the holy silences be lost.
Bow down before the marble Man of Woe,
Bow down before the singing angel host.
What jewelled glory fills my spirit's eye,
What golden grandeur moves the depths of me!
The soaring arches lift me up on high,
Taking my breath with their rare symmetry.

Bow down my soul and let the wondrous light
Of beauty bathe thee from her lofty throne,
Bow down before the wonder of man's might.
Bow down in worship, humble and alone,
Bow lowly down before the sacred sight
Of man's Divinity alive in stone.

BARCELONA

In Barcelona city they dance the nights
Along the streets. The folk, erecting stands
Upon the people's pavements, come together
From pueblo, barrio, in families,
Lured by the lilting playing of the bands,
Rejoicing in the balmy summer weather,
In spreading rings they weave fine fantasies
Like rare mosaics of many-colored lights.

Kindled, it glows, the magical Sardana,
And sweeps the city in a glorious blaze.
The garrison, the sailors from the ships,
The workers join and block the city's ways,
Ripe laughter ringing from intriguing lips,
Crescending like a wonderful hosanna.

II

Oh admirable city from every range!
Whether I stand upon your natural towers,—
With your blue carpet spreading to their feet,
Its patterns undulate between the bars,—
Watching until the tender twilight hours,
Its motion cradling soft a silver fleet;
Or far descend from underneath the stars.

Down—to your bottoms sinister and strange:
The nights eccentric of the Barrio Chino,
The creatures of the shadows of the walls,
Gray like the savage caricatures of Goya,
The chulos of the abysmal dancing halls,
And in the garish lights of La Criolla,
The feminine flamenco of El Niño.

III

Oh Barcelona, queen of Europe's cities,
From dulcet thoughts of you my guts are twisted
With bitter pain of longing for your sights,
And for your hills, your picturesque glory singing,
My feet are mutinous, mine eyes are misted.
Upon my happy thoughts your harbor lights
Are shimmering like bells melodious ringing
With sweet cadenzas of flamenco ditties.

I see your movement flashing like a knife,
Reeling my senses, drunk upon the hues
Of motion, the eternal rainbow wheel,
Your passion smouldering like a lighted fuse,
But more than all sensations, oh I feel
Your color flaming in the dance of life.

Morocco conquering homage paid to Spain
And the Alhambra lifted up its towers!
Africa's fingers tipped with miracles,
And quivering with Arabian designs,
Traced words and figures like exotic flowers,
Sultanas' chambers of rare tapestries,
Filigree marvels from Koranic lines,
Mosaics chanting notes like tropic rain.

And Spain repaid the tribute ages after:
To Tetuan, that fort of struggle and strife,
Where chagrined Andalusian Moors retired,
She brought a fountain bubbling with new life,
Whose jewelled charm won even the native pride,
And filled it sparkling with flamenco laughter.

Oh wistful and heartrending earth, oh land
Of colors singing symphonies of life!
Myself is like a stone upon my spirit,
Reluctant, passing from your sunny shore.
  Oh native colors,
  Pure colors aglow
  With magic light.

Mysterious atmosphere whose elements,
Like hands inspired by a magnetic force,
Touched so caressingly my inmost chords,
How strangely I was brought beneath your spell!
  But willingly
  A captive I
  Remained to be.

Oh friends, my friends! When Ramadan returns
And daily fast and feasting through the night,
With chants and music, honey-dripping sweets,
And fatmahs shaking their flamenco feet,
  My thoughts will wing
  The waves of air
  To be with you.

Oh when the cannon sounds to break the fast,
The children chorus madly their relief,
And you together group to feast at last,
You'll feel my hungry spirit there in your midst,
  Released from me
  A prisoner,
  To fly to you.

And when you go beneath the orange trees,
To mark and serenade the crescent growth,
With droning lute and shivering mandolin,
And drop the scented blossoms in your cups!
     Oh make one tune,
     One melody
     Of love for me.

Keeping your happy vigil through the night,
With tales and music whiling by the hours,
You may recall my joy to be with you,
Until the watchers passed from house to house
     And bugle call
     And muffled drum
     Proclaimed the day!

When liquid-eyed Habeeb draws from the lute
A murmur golden like a thousand bees,
Embowelled in a sheltering tropic tree,
With honey brimming in the honeycomb,
     The tuneful air
     Will waft the sound
     Across to me.

Notes soaked with the dear odor of your soil
And like its water cooling to my tongue,
Haunting me always like a splendid dream,
Of vistas opening to an infinite way
     Of perfect love
     That angels make
     In Paradise.

Habeeb, Habeeba, I may never return
Another sacred fast to keep with you,
But when your Prince of months inaugurates
Our year, my thoughts will turn to Ramadan,
    Forgetting never
    Its tokens
    Unforgettable.

                                —Mektoub.

AMOROSO

ABSENCE

Your words dropped into my heart like pebbles into a pool,
Rippling around my breast and leaving it melting cool.

Your kisses fell sharp on my flesh like dawn-dews from the
limb,
Of a fruit-filled lemon tree when the day is young and dim.

Like soft rain-christened sunshine, as fragile as rare gold lace,
Your breath, sweet-scented and warm, has kindled my tranquil
face.

But a silence vasty-deep, oh deeper than all these ties
Now, through the menacing miles, brooding between us lies.

And more than the songs I sing, I await your written word,
To stir my fluent blood as never your presence stirred.

A RED FLOWER

Your lips are like a southern lily red,
    Wet with soft rain-kisses of the night,
In which the brown bee buries deep its head,
    When still the dawn's a silver sea of light.

Your lips betray the secret of your soul,
    The dark delicious essence that is you,
A mystery of life, the flaming goal
    I seek through mazy pathways strange and new.

Your lips are the red symbol of a dream.
    What visions of warm lilies they impart,
That line the green bank of a fair blue stream,
    With butterflies and bees close to each heart!

Brown bees that murmur sounds of music rare,
    That softly fall upon the languorous breeze,
Wafting them gently on the quiet air
    Among untended avenues of trees.

O were I hovering, a bee, to probe
    Deep down within your scented heart, fair flower,
Enfolded by your soft vermilion robe,
    Amorous of sweets, for but one perfect hour!

TO O.E.A.

Your voice is the color of a robin's breast,
  And there's a sweet sob in it like rain—still rain in the
    night.
Among the leaves of the trumpet-tree, close to his nest,
  The pea-dove sings, and each note thrills me with strange
    delight
Like the words, wet with music, that well from your trembling
    throat.
  I'm afraid of your eyes, they're so bold,
  Searching me through, reading my thoughts, shining like
    gold.
But sometimes they are gentle and soft like the dew on the
    lips of the eucharis
Before the sun comes warm with his lover's kiss.
  You are sea-foam, pure with the star's loveliness,
Not mortal, a flower, a fairy, too fair for the beauty-shorn
    earth.
All wonderful things, all beautiful things, gave of their wealth
    to your birth.
Oh I love you so much, not recking of passion, that I feel it
    is wrong!
  But men will love you, flower, fairy, non-mortal spirit
    burdened with flesh,
Forever, life-long.

ROMANCE

To clasp you now and feel your head close-pressed,
Scented and warm against my beating breast;

To whisper soft and quivering your name,
And drink the passion burning in your frame;

To lie at full length, taut, with cheek to cheek,
And tease your mouth with kisses till you speak

Love words, mad words, dream words, sweet senseless words,
Melodious like notes of mating birds;

To hear you ask if I shall love always,
And myself answer: Till the end of days;

To feel your easeful sigh of happiness
When on your trembling lips I murmur: Yes;

It is so sweet. We know it is not true.
What matters it? The night must shed her dew.

We know it is not true, but it is sweet—
The poem with this music is complete.

The perfume of your body dulls my sense.
  I want nor wine nor weed; your breath alone
Suffices. In this moment rare and tense
  I worship at your breast. The flower is blown,
The saffron petals tempt my amorous mouth,
  The yellow heart is radiant now with dew
Soft-scented, redolent of my loved South;
  O flower of love! I give myself to you.
Uncovered on your couch of figured green,
  Here let us linger indivisible.
The portals of your sanctuary unseen
  Receive my offering, yielding unto me.
Oh, with our love the night is warm and deep!
  The air is sweet, my flower, and sweet the flute
Whose music lulls our burning brain to sleep,
  While we lie loving, passionate and mute.

THE SNOW FAIRY

Throughout the afternoon I watched them there,
Snow-fairies falling, falling from the sky,
Whirling fantastic in the misty air,
Contending fierce for space supremacy.
And they flew down a mightier force at night,
As though in heaven there was revolt and riot,
And they, frail things had taken panic flight
Down to the calm earth seeking peace and quiet.
I went to bed and rose at early dawn
To see them huddled together in a heap,
Each merged into the other upon the lawn,
Worn out by the sharp struggle, fast asleep.
The sun shone brightly on them half the day,
By night they stealthily had stol'n away.

II

And suddenly my thought then turned to you
Who came to me upon a winter's night,
When snow-sprites round my attic window flew,
Your hair disheveled, eyes aglow with light.
My heart was like the weather when you came,
The wanton winds were blowing loud and long;
But you, with joy and passion all aflame,
You danced and sang a lilting summer song.
I made room for you in my little bed,
Took covers from the closet fresh and warm,
A gentle pillow for your scented head,
And lay down with you resting in my arm.
You went with Dawn. You left before the day,
The lonely actor of a dreamy play.

A MEMORY OF JUNE

When June comes dancing on the death of May,
    With scarlet roses tinting her green breast,
And mating thrushes ushering in her day,
    And Earth on tiptoe for her golden guest,

I always see the evening when we met—
    The first of June baptized in tender rain—
And walked home through the wide streets, gleaming wet,
    Arms locked, our warm flesh pulsing with love's pain.

I always see the cheerful little room,
    And in the corner, fresh and white, the bed,
Sweet scented with a delicate perfume,
    Wherein for one night only we were wed;

Where in the starlit stillness we lay mute,
    And heard the whispering showers all night long,
And your brown burning body was a lute
    Whereon my passion played his fevered song.

When June comes dancing on the death of May,
    With scarlet roses staining her fair feet,
My soul takes leave of me to sing all day
    A love so fugitive and so complete.

FLIRTATION

Upon thy purple mat thy body bare
    Is fine and limber like a tender tree.
The motion of thy supple form is rare,
    Like a lithe panther lolling languidly,
Toying and turning slowly in her lair.
        Oh, I would never ask for more of thee,
Thou art so clean in passion and so fair.
        Enough! if thou wilt ask no more of me!

POLARITY

Nay, why reproach each other, be unkind,
    For there's no plane on which we two may meet?
Let's both forgive, forget, for both were blind,
    And life is of a day, and time is fleet.

And I am fire, swift to flame and burn,
    Melting with elements high overhead,
While you are water in an earthly urn,
    All pure, but heavy, and of hue like lead.

TORMENTED

I will not reason, wrestle here with you,
    Though you pursue and worry me about;
As well put forth my swarthy arm to stop
    The wild wind howling, darkly mad without.

The night is yours for revels; day will light.
    I will not fight you, bold and tigerish,
For I am weak, while you are gaining strength;
    Peace! cease tormenting me to have your wish.

But when you're filled and sated with the flesh,
    I shall go swiftly to the silver stream,
To cleanse my body for the spirit's sake,
    And sun my limbs, and close my eyes to dream.

JASMINE

Your scent is in the room.
Swiftly it overwhelms and conquers me!
Jasmine, night jasmine, perfect of perfume,
Heavy with dew before the dawn of day!
Your face was in the mirror. I could see
You smile and vanish suddenly away,
Leaving behind the vestige of a tear.
Sad suffering face, from parting grown so dear!
Night jasmine cannot bloom in this cold place;
Without the street is wet and weird with snow;
The cold nude trees are tossing to and fro;
Too stormy is the night for your fond face;
For your low voice too loud the wind's mad roar.
But oh, your scent is here—jasmines that grow
Luxuriant, clustered round your cottage door!

COMMEMORATION

When first your glory shone upon my face
    My body kindled to a mighty flame,
And burnt you yielding in my hot embrace
    Until you swooned to love, breathing my name.

And wonder came and filled our night of sleep,
    Like a new comet crimsoning the sky;
And stillness like the stillness of the deep
    Suspended lay as an unuttered sigh.

I never again shall feel your warm heart flushed,
    Panting with passion, naked unto mine,
Until the throbbing world around is hushed
    To quiet worship at our scented shrine.

Nor will your glory seek my swarthy face,
    To kindle and to change my jaded frame
Into a miracle of godlike grace,
    Transfigured, bathed in your immortal flame.

MEMORIAL

Your body was a sacred cell always,
    A jewel that grew dull in garish light,
An opal which beneath my wondering gaze
    Gleamed rarely, softly throbbing in the night.

I touched your flesh with reverential hands,
    For you were sweet and timid like a flower
That blossoms out of barren tropic sands,
    Shedding its perfume in one golden hour.

You yielded to my touch with gentle grace,
    And though my passion was a mighty wave
That buried you beneath its strong embrace,
    You were yet happy in the moment's grave.

Still more than passion consummate to me,
    More than the nuptials immemorial sung,
Was the warm thrill that melted me to see
    Your clean brown body, beautiful and young;

The joy in your maturity at length,
    The peace that filled my soul like cooling wine,
When you responded to my tender strength,
    And pressed your heart exulting into mine.

How shall I with such memories of you
    In coarser forms of love fruition find?
No, I would rather like a ghost pursue
    The fairy phantoms of my lonely mind.

ONE YEAR AFTER

Not once in all our days of poignant love,
Did I a single instant give to thee
My undivided being wholly free.
Not all thy potent passion could remove
The barrier that loomed between to prove
The full supreme surrendering of me.
Oh, I was beaten, helpless utterly
Against the shadow-fact with which I strove.
For when a cruel power forced me to face
The truth which poisoned our illicit wine,
That even I was faithless to my race
Bleeding beneath the iron hand of thine,
Our union seemed a monstrous thing and base!
I was an outcast from thy world and mine.

II

Adventure-seasoned and storm-buffeted,
I shun all signs of anchorage, because
The zest of life exceeds the bound of laws.
New gales of tropic fury round my head
Break lashing me through hours of soulful dread;
But when the terror thins and, spent, withdraws,
Leaving me wondering awhile, I pause—
But soon again the risky ways I tread!
No rigid road for me, no peace, no rest,
While molten elements run through my blood;
And beauty-burning bodies manifest
Their warm, heart-melting motions to be wooed;
And passion boldly rising in my breast,
Like rivers of the Spring, lets loose its flood.

FUTILITY

Oh, I have tried to laugh the pain away,
Let new flames brush my love-springs like a feather.
But the old fever seizes me to-day,
As sickness grips a soul in wretched weather.
I have given up myself to every urge,
With not a care of precious powers spent,
Have bared my body to the strangest scourge,
To soothe and deaden my heart's unhealing rent.
But you have torn a nerve out of my frame,
A gut that no physician can replace,
And reft my life of happiness and aim.
Oh what new purpose shall I now embrace?
What substance hold, what lovely form pursue,
When my thought burns through everything to you?

All night, through the eternity of night,
Pain was my portion though I could not feel.
Deep in my humbled heart you ground your heel,
Till I was reft of even my inner light,
Till reason from my mind had taken flight,
And all my world went whirling in a reel.
And all my swarthy strength turned cold like steel,
A passive mass beneath your puny might.
Last night I gave you triumph over me,
So I should be myself as once before,
I marveled at your shallow mystery,
And haunted hungrily your temple door.
I gave you sum and substance to be free,
Oh, you shall never triumph any more!

II

I do not fear to face the fact and say,
How darkly-dull my living hours have grown,
My wounded heart sinks heavier than stone,
Because I loved you longer than a day!
I do not shame to turn myself away
From beckoning flowers beautifully blown,
To mourn your vivid memory alone
In mountain fastnesses austerely gray.
The mists will shroud me on the utter height,
The salty, brimming waters of my breast
Will mingle with the fresh dews of the night
To bathe my spirit hankering to rest.
But after sleep I'll wake with greater might,
Once more to venture on the eternal quest.

THIRST

My spirit wails for water, water now!
My tongue is aching dry, my throat is hot
For water, fresh rain shaken from a bough,
Or dawn dews heavy in some leafy spot.
My hungry body's burning for a swim
In sunlit water where the air is cool,
As in Trout Valley where upon a limb
The golden finch sings sweetly to the pool.
Oh water, water, when the night is done,
When day steals gray-white through the window-pane,
Clear silver water when I wake, alone,
All impotent of parts, of fevered brain;
Pure water from a forest fountain first,
To wash me, cleanse me, and to quench my thirst!

COURAGE

O lonely heart so timid of approach,
    Like the shy tropic flower that shuts its lips
    To the faint touch of tender finger tips:
What is your word? What question would you broach?

Your lustrous-warm eyes are too sadly kind
    To mask the meaning of your dreamy tale,
    Your guarded life too exquisitely frail
Against the daggers of my warring mind.

There is no part of the unyielding earth,
    Even bare rocks where the eagles build their nest,
    Will give us undisturbed and friendly rest.
No dewfall softens this vast belt of dearth.

But in the socket-chiseled teeth of strife,
    That gleam in serried files in all the lands,
    We may join hungry, understanding hands,
And drink our share of ardent love and life.

Books by Claude McKay

available in paperbound editions
from Harcourt Brace Jovanovich, Publishers

BANANA BOTTOM

BANJO

A LONG WAY FROM HOME

SELECTED POEMS OF CLAUDE MCKAY